Original title:
The Locket's Truth

Copyright © 2025 Creative Arts Management OÜ
All rights reserved.

Author: Finn Donovan
ISBN HARDBACK: 978-1-80586-206-2
ISBN PAPERBACK: 978-1-80586-678-7

A Token's Heartfelt Reception

A shiny trinket left behind,
With secrets small, and laughs entwined.
It clinks and clanks upon my chest,
A treasure trove, I must confess.

Inside it holds a note of cheer,
Of silly jokes and puns to share.
Each giggle spills when I take a peek,
A quirky charm that loves to speak.

I wore it once on silly day,
And every glance made folks dismay.
For who would trust a sparkly piece,
To tell a tale that would not cease?

Yet through the laughter, bloopers bloom,
This little charm has found its room.
With every chuckle, joy unfurls,
In this odd heart, where laughter swirls.

The Heart's Enclosure

In a box of shiny gold,
Secrets lie, or so I'm told.
Open it up on a rainy day,
Surprises dance and giggles play.

I thought I'd find a ruby rare,
Instead I found a broken chair.
A paper note has come to light,
It says 'I stole your last bite!'

In the Presence of Silent Witnesses

Hidden gems and trinkets bright,
Each one whispers, oh what a plight!
A sock, a pebble, and a pea,
Crammed inside, all just to see.

I asked the cat, my closest mate,
'What's this mess on my plate?'
He purred and stretched, then looked askance,
'Just pick the fish and take a chance!'

Guardians of the Heart's Stories

There's a bracelet with a teddy's smile,
It guards my tales, stacked in a pile.
A yo-yo spins with every truth,
Rosa's crush from her raucous youth.

A diary dusted, oh what a sight,
Full of crush notes and pillow fights.
Scribbles laugh at past routines,
Secrets hidden behind those scenes!

Echoing Histories Within

Rusty keys and old coins jangle,
Each one sings, no need to wrangle.
They giggle softly, like old friends,
Still making mischief as time bends.

A pair of glasses, thick and round,
They whisper jokes that once were found.
The mirror chuckles, sees it all,
Reflects the past, while we just sprawl!

Enigmatic Keepsakes in the Dark

In a drawer, treasures hide,
Brass buttons, an old shoe tie.
Dust bunnies dance, a cheeky lot,
What's in here? Well, I forgot.

A spoon that's bent, a mystery brew,
Did I really love that blue?
A rubber chicken, such delight,
Who knew it could cause a fright?

The Weight of Nostalgic Gold

A necklace tangled, a laugh I make,
Next to a photo of a dog named Jake.
A chipped mug whispers tales of cheer,
I wonder if ghosts sip coffee here?

Old coins jingle, far too grand,
Where'd I stash my talent and band?
In a pocket, oddities do dwell,
Is that a secret? Who can tell?

Heartfelt Echoes of Adornment

Rings of plastic, colors bright,
Worn by kids, a silly sight.
A necklace strung with jellybeans,
Was that my style or just dreams?

A charm made from an old fish hook,
Do I keep it? Well, let's look!
Grandma's pearls, once so prime,
Now just a punchline, what a crime!

Beyond the Surface of Time

An old watch ticks, or maybe snores,
It knows the time, but not the chores.
A funky hat, a feathered spree,
Who wore this? Not sure it's me!

Beneath the bed, a sock brigade,
Arguing over who gets laid.
Memories clash, a playful blurt,
In this chaos, love won't hurt!

Shadows of a Delicate Promise

In a box of dust and dreams,
A hidden gem shines bright and beams.
It whispers tales both odd and strange,
Of love, of loss, and silly change.

With every twist, a giggle springs,
A dance of shadows, flapping wings.
Promises made, like socks that mismatch,
Laughter rings out with each little catch.

Through winks and jinks, the truth's revealed,
With every grin, the heart is healed.
What once was serious, now a jest,
In laughter's arms, we find our rest.

So hold it close, that trinket rare,
With a chuckle, toss away despair.
For in its clasp, the punchlines freeze,
In shadows bright, we're sure to tease.

The Pendant's Silent Song

A pendant hangs with words unspoken,
Its silence sings, yet none are broken.
What mysteries lie in its shiny face,
With tales that giggle at a quickened pace?

A spin, a twirl, it spins around,
Telling secrets from the underground.
Jokes about cats and unexpected fall,
The laughs unfold and peace calls all.

With each small jingle, joy awakes,
A necklace that giggles, oh, the stakes!
Soon enough, we'll know its jest,
Life's little quirks, we're truly blessed.

So wear it proud, let laughter reign,
In every glance, joy will remain.
For in its glow, the fun won't cease,
A silent song that brings us peace.

Time's Embrace in a Charm

A charm that ticks with glee untold,
In its embrace, the funniest gold.
It hugs the moments, some quite absurd,
A blend of giggles and whispered words.

With every hour, a quirky quirk,
It dances like a mobile clerk.
Time leaps back with a cheerful bound,
And life's best punchlines all around.

Each tick a wink, a playful tease,
It jests with time like a summer breeze.
So let it clasp, both bold and bright,
For laughter shares its lovely light.

Embrace the charm, let worries far,
In every tick, find who you are.
For in this joy, the day will gleam,
Time's embrace is just a dream.

Reflections in Precious Metal

In polished shine, reflections bloom,
With silly faces crafted from gloom.
What quirks arise when silver gleams,
And every glance unleashes dreams?

A mirror held to laughter bright,
It bends the truth in pure delight.
Oh shiny trinkets, double the fun,
When jokes collide, we come undone.

With every shout, a sparkle plays,
In precious metal, the humor stays.
Twists of fate dance through the night,
We'll laugh until the morning light.

So catch the glint, embrace the jest,
In gleaming smiles, we're truly blessed.
For laughter's charm, in gleams and shades,
Reflects the joy that never fades.

The Enigma of Locked Hearts

In a box, a heart-shaped prize,
With a twist and a little surprise.
I opened it wide, oh what a sight,
A sock? A cat? That can't be right!

Secrets sealed in glimmering lore,
A note from grandma, 'Please vacuum more!'
Whispers of love or a joke gone wrong,
This trinket dances but doesn't belong.

Beneath the Outer Shell

A shiny case with many a flair,
Hiding treasures, if I dare.
Is this a memory or just my lunch?
Peanut butter? What a funny crunch!

Tales of yore mixed in with crumbs,
A note that reads 'Beware of chums!'
Were there hearts, or just spilled tea?
Who knew a bauble could hold so much glee?

Wearer of Secrets Untold

A pendant draped upon my neck,
A mystery wrapped in a techy fleck.
What's inside, a tear or a joke?
A riddle awaits, or just a poke?

Each clink and clank's a tale to tell,
Of epic fails and chores gone well.
A giggle trapped in this wild charm,
Check it out, cause it's got real charm!

Stories Etched in Silver

In silver, they etched their dreams so bright,
But what's this? A cat's hair in sight?
A yearbook pic? Or grandma's phone?
Did I join a club I didn't own?

Each curve holds echoes, laughs, and sighs,
Even old lists of unmade pies.
A heart, a bellyache, or just my luck?
In the chaos, who needs to pluck?

Reverberations of a Silent Bond

In a pocket, small and round,
A secret place where laughs abound.
Hidden jokes and silly quirks,
A treasure trove that subtly lurks.

With a wink and a knowing glance,
We share a smile, a quiet dance.
When silence speaks, we hear it loud,
A bond so strong, we're both so proud.

Each whisper soft, a chuckle bright,
In playful pranks, we take delight.
A note that folds, a hairpin twist,
The things we share, how could we miss?

In silly hats, we grace the town,
With our shenanigans, we won't frown.
Our laughter echoes, soft but clear,
In this odd world, we hold so dear.

The Essence of what Lies Within

A trinket glints, a wink of fate,
It holds the truth of our debate.
With every joke, it feels just right,
To twist the plot, then take to flight.

A flick, a twirl, a daring spin,
In playful jest, where do we begin?
The silly faces, the clumsy falls,
We make a scene in crowded halls.

With gummy bears and soda pop,
We craft our world with every swap.
A mix-up here, a slip on cue,
The essence of me, is deeply you.

In every giggle, a hint of glee,
We savor time, wild and free.
This secret game we always play,
Keeps dullness at a far-away.

Remnants of Lost Conversations

In echoes faint, old tales we spin,
With playful words and cheeky grins.
Forgotten chats, they linger still,
In awkward pauses, we find the thrill.

A mix of laughter, a slice of cake,
Old stories shared, for humor's sake.
What once was serious, now feels absurd,
In fading light, we stumble, unheard.

A paper plane, it soars and dives,
Rescue missions for lost archives.
In cryptic notes, we plot our schemes,
A canvas bright, we're painting dreams.

With each mishap, our bond grows tight,
In jumbled words, we find the light.
In the remnants of what we said,
Lies a treasure as we laugh ahead.

Timeless Threads of Connection

With silly strings, we tie our fate,
In knots of joy, we celebrate.
Each thread a story, a stitch of fun,
In wild confusion, we're never done.

As laughter threads through every seam,
We weave our world, a playful dream.
In winks and nudges, we dance around,
Creating moments, laughter found.

In mismatched socks, we strut the line,
In tangled tales, our hearts entwine.
A game of quirks, we can't resist,
In every twist, our fun persists.

Through ups and downs, we hold the thread,
In timeless tales, no words unsaid.
A tapestry of laughs we'll make,
In this grand play, there's no mistake.

A Jewel's Hidden Narrative

In a drawer, a trinket lies,
Chasing dust with winkless eyes.
It once brought joy, or so they say,
Now it just laughs at disarray.

Caught in tales of love and fate,
It fumbles dates, can't keep straight.
A brooch turned ring? Oh, what a mess!
Who knew fashion could cause such stress?

Legacy Woven in Gold

A chain of blunders, oh so bright,
Gifted with glee, wrapped up tight.
Unraveled stories, a tangled thread,
Makes family gatherings quite widespread.

A cousin's faux pas, an uncle's joke,
Each time they chuckle, the past's bespoke.
The shiny charm, a family lore,
Hides a past that we can't ignore.

Cursed Keepsake

A dusty relic with a glinting stare,
Claims to hold secrets, but lacks a care.
Whispers of doom in a shiny hue,
Turns out it's just a bad egg or two.

Each owner flees, with a hasty laugh,
Thinking of fortune but facing the wrath.
A compass that points every which way,
Leading lost souls to a comedy play.

Blessed Reminiscence

A mirror of jest from days of yore,
Reflecting antics and tales galore.
Nana's pearls, a slippery prize,
Always a giggle, with dubious ties.

In wedding photos, a whimsy shown,
Each showed off in a comical tone.
Smiles and photos that come alive,
Even in chaos, that's how we thrive!

Glimpses of Yesterday's Embrace

In time's embrace, a jester's role,
Dances of past, a misfit soul.
Old socks as gifts, what a delight!
A vintage shoe, just not quite right.

Each memory sparkles with a grin,
We remember the laughter beneath the skin.
Through silly moments, we all align,
In forgotten treasures, we find the shine.

The Circle of What We Cherish

In a circle, we gather tight,
With trinkets that shine so bright.
A hairpin, a button, a shoelace too,
Can spark laughter – who knew?

We take turns sharing our prized,
Like a cat with its quirky size.
Last week's sock, it still has its smell,
In this odd treasure, we find our spell.

What's shared is odd, that's for sure,
But the giggles and snickers, they simply allure.
A misfit's gold tucked in with glee,
In this circle of joy, just let it be!

So here's to the things we love to keep,
They make us chuckle, they make us leap.
In laughter we discover our bonds are true,
With each silly trinket, a memory skewed.

Glances Stowed in a Heartfelt Artifact

Within this box where treasures rest,
A sock that dances, who'd have guessed?
A rubber chicken, a giggle's delight,
In this charm, we find our light.

With every glance, a story unfolds,
Of last summer's crush, or adventures bold.
And that loose tooth, from ages ago,
Incites laughter, reminisce as we go.

A button that sparkles with a wink,
Reminds us of soda and brightly pink drink.
A rubber band stretched beyond its prime,
In our Artifact, it's always a good time.

So stash your glances in this quirky space,
For memories shared, they'll never erase.
With each cheeky note or peculiar find,
We cherish the laughs left far behind.

Secrets Beneath the Surface

Beneath the surface, whispers dwell,
Of hairy secrets, we know too well.
A sandwich crust from a year ago,
In this odd pot, the tales will grow.

What lies beneath? Oh, take a peek!
A carrot or two, though maybe weak.
A sock that traveled far and wide,
In this treasure chest, it basks with pride.

Each curious find pulls grins from us,
What a ridiculous, rollicking fuss!
Old candy wrappers, they've got charm,
In these sweet secrets, we feel their warmth.

So dip in deep if you dare explore,
What's hiding beneath will leave you wanting more.
With silly surprises wrapped tight in a beat,
Let's giggle along and feel their heartbeat!

Whispers of Hidden Memories

In a quiet space, whispers call,
Of forgotten laughter, we've stored them all.
A wobbly toy that giggles with glee,
Holds ticklish tales, just wait and see.

A postcard from a trip gone awry,
With doodles of cows and a bright blue sky.
We fashion a story with each flip and fold,
Memories hidden, just waiting to unfold.

Each secret layer paves the way,
For chuckles on this bright-hearted day.
Bits of color, threads of delight,
Turn missing socks into a comical sight.

So gather the whispers, let laughter swell,
In every corner, a joyous tale to tell.
With hidden treasures, let's dance with glee,
In this tapestry of cherished memory!

The Guardian of Longing Hearts

In a pocket it rests, quite snug and tight,
A trinket of wishes, by day and night.
Who knew such a thing could cause a fuss?
It holds all the secrets, just waiting for us.

A glance in its glass, a flirty little wink,
Wondering what heart, in twirls, must think.
It giggles and giggles, oh, what a tease!
Every lover's dream wrapped up with ease.

With a jingle and jangle, it dances around,
Singing of romances, joyfully found.
But be wary, dear friend, for fate takes a leap,
When the truth of its charm puts your heart in a heap.

Oh, carrying treasures both big and small,
Can lead to confusion or even a brawl.
So keep it close by, let laughter be heard,
For the guardian's laughter is never absurd!

Between Each Link, a Story

In a chain so shiny, stories unwind,
Of clumsy romances, and love that's blind.
With each little link, a blunder unfolds,
And giggles erupt as the tale slowly rolls.

There's a clink from the past of a dinner gone wrong,
A spaghetti mishap turned into a song.
Each segment revealing a comedic delight,
Of tangled-up hearts that just can't stay tight.

Oh, the laughs that it carries, the joy that it brings,
A saga of snickers, like musical rings.
In the twists and turns, there's no need to pout,
For in every mishap, true love carries out.

So hold it up high, let the sunshine in,
Each link a reminder of how love can win.
Through kinks and shenanigans, all dressed in gold,
The warmest of stories together unfold.

Whispered Vows Frozen in Time

A vow tucked away, in glitter and shine,
With giggles of lovers, both silly and fine.
It promises laughter, and perhaps a small brawl,
As their secret confessions bounce off the wall.

In the chill of the night, two hearts make a pact,
To share all their dreams, but forget all the fact.
With whispers so saucy, it brightens the gloom,
As the chilly night air becomes love's own room.

A moment preserved, with a wink and a nod,
In a freeze-frame of joy, they both fit the squad.
With puns and with pitter-pats filling the air,
Every laugh generates the sweetest affair.

So here's to the vows, both comical and true,
Crafted in laughter, with a twist just for two.
For frozen in time, those giggles resound,
Unraveling stories where love can be found.

Love Encased in Gilded Shadows

In shadows that dance, love jests and it spins,
Cloaked in a shimmer where laughter begins.
A box full of chuckles, twinkling at night,
Whispers and giggles, what a marvelous sight.

The secrets it keeps, oh, they're just such a tease,
Of romps through the park, and giggles that please.
With every glance inward, a smile does bloom,
As they ponder the treasure held in this room.

Oh, the gilded allure can fool you, it's true,
For laughter can turn, and leave love askew.
Yet still they will cherish each vibrant endeavor,
For hidden delights make their love last forever.

So let shadows dance, let the jokes explode,
For love's peak adventure is the best of the road.
Tucked away nicely, each giggle's a thrill,
In gilded enclosure, it brings such a chill.

Memories Captured in Chains

A locket spins with tales untold,
Of secret crushes and kisses bold.
Photos inside, a bit askew,
Blurry faces, who even knew?

Dancing shoes from times long past,
Each memory stuck, a glimpse so fast.
Locked away with a twist and a turn,
Who'd wish to see those fashion burns?

Each snap a laugh, a mock parade,
Who wore that hat in the summer shade?
A grin so wide, it's hard to tell,
If love or laughter cast the spell.

So grab your keys, let's take a peek,
Into wild days that seem so sleek.
What's hidden there, only you can share,
With snacks in hand, let's shred despair!

The Portrait of the Unspoken

In a frame of laughter, secrets hide,
Chubby cheeks of a childhood pride.
Faces once fresh, now set in dust,
A sibling's smirk, a witness must!

Tickling toes in a goofy dance,
Who knew that smile could take a chance?
Captured moments of total glee,
What does this portrait say of me?

Hats on heads, a mismatched spree,
Was that a banana or monkey's knee?
A snapshot caught of pure delight,
But the truth is, we missed the light!

So let's unearth those giggles tucked,
In frames of gold, we are plucked.
With stories swirling 'round like steam,
In this unspoken, we create a dream!

Between Two Hearts, a Silent Echo

Between two beats, a secret hum,
In whispers soft, my heart goes thrum.
A tale of silly, a comedic twist,
Oh, what you missed, it can't be kissed!

Puppy love made us all cringe,
Sent notes in class, a little fringed.
We passed the love like it was hot,
But awkwardness was all we got!

Hearts like jellybeans, sweet and bright,
One could tangle in sheer delight.
But oops! That moment fell so flat,
When Cupid's arrow turned to a cat!

In silent echoes, we now reside,
With chuckles shared, and arms opened wide.
Between those beats, we hold the key,
To laughter's door, just you and me!

Echoes in a Hidden Chamber

In chambers deep, where echoes play,
A raucous laugh lights up the day.
Secrets linger in corners bright,
Of goofy moments and fears in flight.

Glimpses of tomfoolery, grins displayed,
A secret stash of antics laid.
From toe socks to shoes of two-tone,
Each snapshot finds its place to roam.

A feathered hat and a clownish grin,
Underneath, we all dive in!
Collecting chuckles like fancy pies,
Spilling joy where memory lies.

So let's frolic in this hidden nook,
And dust off those tales in every book.
With echoes ringing, we're not alone,
In this chamber of mischief, we've happily grown!

Love's Echo in Metal Form

In a shiny circle lies a tale,
Where laughter dances, never pale.
A heart-shaped charm, a wobbly dance,
Reminding us of a comical chance.

With each jingle, a chuckle spills,
Echoes of love, with silly thrills.
A secret whisper in playful guise,
Tales of romance and awkward sighs.

Between the clasp, a giggle hides,
A story of love where humor abides.
Tangled in metal, a whimsical twist,
Oh, did I mention that hug on the list?

So spin the locket, let joy unfurl,
Unlock the giggles that make us twirl.
For in its heart, mischief awaits,
A funny reminder of love's silly traits.

The Secret Within the Heart's Frame

Behind the frame, a secret awaits,
Full of giggles, not just nice dates.
A hidden note, signed with a pun,
Love wrapped in laughter, oh what fun!

When opened wide, what a surprise,
A snapshot of silly, oh how it pries!
Ticklish moments trapped inside,
Mirthful mischief, love's funny ride.

In this frame, the heartbeats grin,
Caught in a moment, oh where to begin?
With every glance, a chuckle lifts,
A treasure chest filled with humorous gifts.

So clasp it tight, let no one see,
The whimsical secrets inside of me.
For love's frame hides a playful start,
A hilarious truth, dear to the heart.

Captured Moments in Silver

In silver's grasp, the moments shine,
Captured laughter, cozy and fine.
Each twist and turn, a tickle inside,
Silly embraces, where we can't hide.

A picture snapped at the perfect time,
With goofy faces, it feels like a rhyme.
Every reflection a giggling spree,
Holding memories of you and me.

Within these edges, a riot of cheer,
Moments sealed that bring us near.
With every glimmer, a funny face,
Reminders of joy, a charming space.

So shake it gently, let it all show,
The silver's secrets, not just so-so.
For in this pendant, love does partake,
In captured moments, with laughter at stake.

The Puzzle of Precious Keepsakes

In a tiny box, bits and baubles reside,
A funny puzzle where quirks coincide.
Each piece a memory, clumsy and bright,
Laughing in silence, day and night.

Searching for gems that sparkle and gleam,
Like odd little dreams that make us beam.
Half a ticket, a lost shoe's pair,
Whimsical treasures show we do care.

A mix of laughter, a clumsy twist,
Every keepsake tells tales we can't resist.
A button, a straw, oh what a mess,
Stitched together in laughter, I guess.

So when mysteries wrap in fantastic noise,
Remember the fun, the goofy joys.
For these puzzling keepsakes, so sweetly designed,
Unravel a story of love intertwined.

Unspoken Sentiments Encased

In a little box, so shiny and bright,
Secrets and giggles hiding from sight.
Whispers of love, with a hint of a jest,
A treasure so silly, it's simply the best.

A photograph trapped in a snap of pure glee,
What's up with that hair? Oh dear, let it be!
Beyond the sweet laughter, lies a quirky embrace,
In this heart-shaped frame, all worries displaced.

In the Grasp of Sentimental Treasures

A bauble so cheesy, it clings like a friend,
Within its fine clasp, the fun doesn't end.
A doodle from school and a note with a grin,
Reminders of moments where silliness wins.

Tickles and giggles in every small fold,
Catch me if you can, it's a memory hold!
Wrapped up in laughter, it's moments like these,
That hold on forever with whimsical ease.

Hearts Entwined in Metal

Two hearts in the metal, quite tangled and sweet,
Like cats in a box, they dance to a beat.
Beneath little arches, their secrets entwine,
With chuckles and snickers that sparkle and shine.

Doodles and jokes carved deep with a grin,
A promise of laughter, let the fun begin!
Hiding in shadows, they wink and they pry,
This shiny romance makes poodles fly high.

Fragments of a Lost Time

Glimmers of moments, both silly and rare,
Gathering dust while they dance in the air.
A comb from a trip, never used, but a gem,
Whispers of laughter, where dreams start to stem.

Tick-tock goes the clock, but we're lost in a spin,
Invented our tales of the chaos within.
In a treasure so daft, what secrets we boast,
A laugh from the past, it's what we love most.

Beneath the Chain

A shiny thing hangs on my neck,
I lost it twice, oh what the heck!
My cat thinks it's a shiny toy,
He pounces around with endless joy.

It holds secrets of old and new,
Like my grandma's false teeth, it's true!
They didn't fit, but what a sight,
Every time she laughed, it was quite a fright.

A photo hidden, a funky face,
Wearing socks in a special place!
I chuckle each time I take a peek,
Who would have thought her style was so chic?

Now it swings when I dance around,
A clanky tune, a silly sound!
With every sway, I feel the glee,
Who knew old charms could set me free?

A Tale Unraveled

In a box of memories piled high,
I found a trinket that caught my eye.
It squeaks when squeezed, this little gem,
Is that a secret? I just can't stem!

Around my neck, it graces me,
A story twisted like a spaghetti spree.
It whispers tales of pizza nights,
And birthday brawls with silly fights.

Every time I wear it out,
Do people think I'm full of clout?
But really, it's just a fancy joke,
Like wearing socks with sandals - yoke!

My friends all laugh and roll their eyes,
As I parade with wacky pride.
Each glance at me causes a snicker,
Guess silly moments, they just grow thicker!

Unveiling Shadows of the Past

A trinket trapped in the dusty chest,
What could it be? Just take a guess!
I opened it up with a creaky sound,
A rubber chicken is what I found!

It once belonged to cousin Lou,
Whose antics always made us blue.
But now it quacks, with flair so grand,
Bringing smiles across the land.

Tangled tales wrapped in a knot,
Like grandma's stories that hit the spot.
I wear it proud, my feathered crown,
In a world of frowns, I'll never drown!

So here's to laughter, stored in charm,
A goofy keepsake, a lucky balm.
Let's share the joy with silly pride,
For laughter's glow, we will abide!

The Treasure Beneath the Skin

I found a charm that's bright and bold,
A little treasure, or so I'm told.
It tickles me when it's close at hand,
Like knowing it's there - a vibrant band.

It jingles when I dance about,
Makes my friends laugh, shout, and sprout.
With each sly move, it brings delight,
Like a squirrel sneaking snacks at night.

At times it hides in my funny sock,
A mystery that no one can unlock!
But when it's found in midday sun,
We giggle out loud, it's all in fun!

So here's to trinkets that make us smile,
With memories sweet, they're worth the while.
For laughter is the treasure we seek,
With every chuckle, life feels unique.

In the Grip of Memory's Embrace

A necklace gleams, a riddle profound,
What stories lie in this little round?
I twist it here, I twist it there,
My hamster thinks it's a comfy chair!

I wore it once to a fancy ball,
But what I spilled was the real downfall.
A whole plate of spaghetti gone astray,
Now it's a snack for my furry bay!

A frozen moment from days gone by,
It winks at me with a cheeky eye.
"Oh, dear!" it seems to say with glee,
"Let's make more stories, just you and me!"

With wobbly steps, we tread along,
In this crazy dance, we both belong.
For life's a jest, with laughter we embrace,
In this wild ride, we find our place!

Bonded by the Weight of Time

A trinket hangs, oh what a sight,
Hiding secrets, feeling light.
It jangles 'round with each odd move,
I swear it's got a groove!

Dusty memories stuck like glue,
Of clumsy hugs and a pet parakeet too.
It laughs at past mishaps, oh so bold,
In this little case, the stories unfold!

Yet when I wear it, folks just stare,
"Is that a charm or a cat's old hair?"
But I beam with pride, a love so neat,
This weight of time, I won't admit defeat!

So here's to relics, both tacky and grand,
They carry laughter, even a band.
In every clasp, there's a silly tale,
Bonded by time's amusing trail!

Eyes that See Beyond the Frame

Tiny glass panes in a silver case,
They peek at love with a curious face.
Two prying eyes from the days gone by,
They giggle at my lil' butterfly!

They've witnessed blunders, a fruit fight fling,
Whispers of love, oh, the joy they bring!
With every glance, they seem to grin,
"Remember that time you fell in the bin?"

With winks and wiggles, they tease and play,
As I faff about, trying to save the day.
Who needs a therapist when you've got this pair,
Eyes that share laughter beyond compare!

Forever capturing moments so quaint,
These tiny spies, they rarely faint.
In their gaze, fun memories glint,
A treasure chest of giggles that never stint!

Ties that Bind Through Adornments

Links of metal and beads that gleam,
Bumping together like a dream team.
They fumble and jangle with every chance,
Oh, the mischief in this merry dance!

Charmed with humor, they clink and chime,
Binding us through the ties of time.
Each little bauble, a story to tell,
Like the time I tripped and fell down the well!

In gatherings, they steal the show,
With jingles that keep the laughter flow.
Who knew adornments held such mirth?
Proving that fun is our greatest worth!

Forever tangled with giggles so fab,
Creating chaos like a jolly tab.
These ties we wear, an amusing design,
In every sparkle, our spirits align!

A Memory Close to the Heart

Nestled within, a charm, a laugh,
Reminds me of that wacky half-and-half.
With a twist of fate, it came to be,
A memory close, like a buzzing bee!

It whispers tales of ice cream spills,
And wonky dance moves that gave me chills.
From picnics gone wrong to moments of glee,
This trinket sings our history!

In cluttered drawers, it shines so bright,
Wrapped in joy, it feels just right.
Each ding and scratch tells a funny tale,
A testament to fun that will never pale!

So here's to the bauble full of cheer,
Holding memories that draw us near.
Close to my heart, it will remain,
A comical bond that will never wane!

A Charm that Binds

In the drawer, a trinket lies,
A charm that holds a great surprise.
It giggles softly, makes me grin,
Tales of mishaps hidden within.

The cat jumped high, knocked it askew,
Thought it was a mouse, so true!
Chasing shadows, all around,
It tumbled down to the ground.

A memory held in tiny clinks,
Of tea parties and midnight drinks.
It whispers lightly as I wear,
A charm that keeps my laughter rare.

So here I laugh while it spins tales,
Of clumsy dances and funny fails.
In every twist, a chuckle found,
Bound together, joy abounds.

Reflections in the Heart's Mirror

I glance at me, but what is this?
A face that wears a comical bliss.
Those freckles giggle, the smile wide,
A reflection where humor does abide.

In every wrinkle, a joke is drawn,
A story told from dusk till dawn.
Oh, what a face full of delight,
Winking back with glee each night.

The mirror winks, "You silly thing,
Who knew you had a crown to bring?"
With laughter bursting, I can't resist,
Embracing joy, I raise my fist.

So here I stand, a jester proud,
Dancing dreams, oh, laugh aloud!
In every glance, a new tale's spun,
Reflections that make my heart run fun.

A Thread Woven Through Time

Once was a thread, so bright and bold,
Woven through tales, adventures told.
It tangled twice with socks and shoes,
A laughter quilt, there's nothing to lose.

As grandma stitched with humor's grace,
The yarn would skip, all over the place.
"Oops!" she'd say, never a frown,
Every knot wore a little crown.

Years twisted on, yet here we are,
A mischievous thread, a shining star.
It plays hide and seek, a grand parade,
Master of pranks that never fade.

In every stitch, a chuckle's found,
With yarn so wild, my heart is bound.
The memories dance like kids on a rhyme,
A timeless tale, a funny climb.

The Keeper's Silent Promise

A jar on the shelf holds secrets tight,
Promises whispered in the dim light.
It chuckles softly when opened wide,
With every giggle, there's joy inside.

A humble keeper of laughter rare,
Each sound a spark of sunshine to share.
Oh, what mischief did you hide?
A symphony of fun, moonlit pride.

Its lid will dance when dreams take flight,
Hopscotch stories skip into the night.
"Oh, remember when?" it playfully shouts,
Keep it together when laughter droughts.

For every promise, a tickle here,
A chuckle shared in love so near.
In the silence, let joy rise high,
The keeper holds laughter, we can't deny.

Within the Circle of Eternity

A trinket round, on a string so fine,
Holds secrets of love, oh how divine!
Could it jumpstart romance, or cause a mess?
With a wink and a grin, I must confess.

In olden days, it slipped from my grip,
Rolling down hallways, a comical trip.
Chasing it fast, dodging a shoe,
Until it stopped, howling, 'What's wrong with you?'

It whispered sweet nothings, made me chuckle,
As I pondered if it would make my heart buckle.
Yet with each twist, it spilled all the beans,
Syncing my love life to sitcom scenes.

So here's to the charm, the mischief it brings,
Wrapping us both in its curious strings.
In circles so wild, where giggles won't cease,
Eternity's fun, may we dance in peace!

Tales Adrift in a Gilded Frame

A shiny old frame, where the tales reside,
Filled with goofy faces, all wearing pride.
Yet what stories lurk beneath the sheen?
Hilarity buried, waiting to be seen.

Once a picture fell, break-dancing in air,
Caught my great aunt doing the robot flair.
Her locket doubled as a disco ball,
Lighting up rooms, oh it dazzled us all!

Then there's Uncle Joe, a romantic tease,
With a photo that captured his biggest cheese.
In love with a pie, oh what a sight,
He claimed it was love at first bite, pure delight!

So tales in this frame, like jellybeans burst,
Each story uproarious, quenching my thirst.
With laughter afloat, we toast to the game,
Of tales adrift, in a gilded frame!

The Chained Heart's Paradox

A heart on a chain, well that sounds nice,
But wait, what if it's full of bad advice?
Chained to the sofa, watching TV's glow,
Dreaming of adventure, with popcorn in tow.

My friend claims it's magic, a love charm indeed,
Yet every date ends with 'You'll never succeed!'
What's more puzzling than this heart on a chain?
Why does it attract all the wrong kind of pain?

Around every twist, there's giggles galore,
As it drags my hopes across the kitchen floor.
With every tug, I trip and I fall,
Into love's wild dance, where I might lose it all!

But let's not forget the joy it brings,
With each funny tale, my soul it sings.
In the paradox found, with a wink and a smirk,
Chained heart or not, I still do the work!

A Charm of Forgotten Vows

A tiny charm sits, tucked in a drawer,
Forgotten like socks, from a discount store.
Once promised romance, now dust-covered fate,
It giggles and grins, laughing at date rate.

Once a party piece, it danced with the moon,
Mended my heart, like a goofy cartoon.
But now it just snoozes, what's in store?
A chance for a chuckle, or a snooze once more?

It whispers of vows, or perhaps just a joke,
Of promises made, like an old-fashioned poke.
"Remember that time?" it teases with glee,
As it rolls off the table, crashing on me!

So here's to the charm, cheers to its reign,
Mixing the real with that silly old strain.
In moments quite strange, where laughter can thrive,
We toast to the whims that keep the heart alive!

When Time Rests in a Small Space

In a pocket it sneezes, just out of sight,
A timepiece once loud, now whispers delight.
Tick-tock giggles while hiding away,
Waiting for moments to join in the play.

With a dance of the hands, it shimmies with glee,
Turning seconds to minutes, just wait and see!
It whispers of lunchtime and naps in the sun,
While sharing its secrets, oh what foolish fun!

Wrap it in stories, all jumbled and tossed,
This small space of time knows not what it lost.
With a wink at the cheese, it's ready to play,
Holding laughter in tickles that never decay.

So cherish the chaos, the moments so cheeky,
Where time likes to frolic, not just feeling sneaky.
In a pocket it thrives, this cheeky delight,
Whispering secrets 'til day turns to night.

The Silent Witness of Adoration

A trinket so small, yet packed full of dreams,
Whispers of blushes and wide silly beams.
It watches the kisses, the winks in the dark,
As love plays its symphony, carving a spark.

In dance halls of day, and the night's gentle sway,
This quiet observer just giggles away.
Counting the moments, an innocent spy,
As creams get spilled and sweets tempt the shy.

It's a topper of stories, a collector of sighs,
With laughter like rainbows and mischief that flies.
So remember it watches, all secrets it keeps,
While love dips in chocolate and innocence leaps.

In the chaos of passion, there's one thing to know,
This locket still smiles at the highs and the lows.
With a twist and a turn, and a playful little shine,
It holds the sweet moments — oh, how they divine!

Charms of Forgotten Love

In a drawer stuffed with receipts and old fluff,
Lies a charm of great dreams and equally tough.
It jingles and jangles, aired out just right,
Stirring up laughter while hiding from light.

Each charm holds a tale, a hiccup or two,
Of crushes and blunders, each silly and true.
From hearts made of candy to notes gone astray,
It's a candy jar's echo of love's grand ballet.

With each gentle jostle, it dances with flair,
Recalling sweet giggles that floated on air.
Though long lost to time, the joy still remains,
In the dances of memories, love's jolly refrains.

So cherish these tokens, with warmth they will bring,
A souvenir's promise that makes your heart sing.
For love comes in trinkets, in laughter and cheer,
In the charms of the past, all the joy's always near.

A Pendant of Stories Untold

Hanging from necks where giggles collide,
Is a pendant of stories, no place left to hide.
Each jingle and jangle, a laugh yet unsaid,
Twinkling with mischief like crumbs of warm bread.

It whispers of wishes — oh, dreams made of dew,
Of breadcrumbs on paths that we often pursue.
A feather from pillows where snores start to play,
And memories rain down like the sun's warm ray.

Tucked in the folds of a daydreamer's heart,
This pendant just spins, a mystical art.
With secrets so vibrant, it lights up a room,
Through giggles and chuckles, it dares to assume.

So wear it with pride, let your laughter be bold,
A pendant of stories, forever retold.
In the giggles of life that we gather and weave,
Are the dreams we hold tight, and the fun we perceive.

Treasures of the Heart's Record

In a box of sparkles and dust,
I found a charm, that I must,
Whispering secrets of love long past,
Like a storybook that couldn't last.

It jinks and jangles, quite the show,
A giggle here, a chuckle low,
It tells of crushes and silly tears,
Of laughs and fumbles throughout the years.

Oh, what a tale in shiny guise,
Of dreamers lost in starry skies,
A treasure trove held close to heart,
A giggle box that plays its part.

So here's to memories, light and dear,
Each trinket sparkles, brings a cheer,
In metal dreams, our laughter grew,
Chasing shadows of love, it's true!

In the Embrace of Metal and Memory

Twinkling metal, what's your deal?
You hold my laughter, you spin and reel,
Each dent and scratch tells a joke,
Of late-night snacks and silly stoke.

Wrapped around my neck so tight,
You've seen my dance moves, what a sight!
A waltz of whimsy, a shaky spin,
With every twirl, the giggles begin.

Oh memories, like bubbles, rise,
In this embrace where laughter lies,
Each twist of fate, a comedy,
In your clasp, I feel so free.

So let us laugh at times gone by,
In shiny metal, under the sky,
With every jingle, hearts take flight,
In memories wrapped, pure delight!

A Dance of Time and Longing

Oh, the stories you've seen unfold,
An dance of time, a heart of gold,
Each twist and turn adds to your tale,
With every laugh, you never fail.

I wore you during the silly parade,
With mismatched socks, I felt quite swayed,
You jingled loud, like a laugh on cue,
In every step, my joy just grew.

Memories swirling, like leaves in fall,
Through time's mishaps, I recall,
Each blunder turned into a grin,
In your company, I dared to spin.

Forever you'll be my shiny muse,
A dance of longing that I choose,
With laughs and quirks, life feels so bright,
In the rhythm of joy, we take flight!

Intricate Patterns of Memory

Oh, look at you! So twisted and fine,
A patchwork of giggles, memories intertwine,
Each loop a riddle, a jesting pout,
In intricate patterns, let's laugh it out.

You've seen the bloopers, the slips, the falls,
The joys of triumph, the echoing calls,
Each glance brings back a ticklish cheer,
In your intricate weave, memories near.

So here's to fun, in every line,
To moments that sparkle, purely divine,
In the chaos of life, you dance with grace,
An entwined story, a memorable embrace.

With each twist and turn, oh can't you see?
You hold the laughter that sets us free,
In patterns of folly, joy find its way,
In the tapestry of life, forever we play!

Whispers of Hidden Memories

In a little round charm, old tales reside,
Hiding giggles and secrets, oh what a ride!
It clinks with my laughter, a dress-up delight,
Whispering stories when the moon's shining bright.

A twist of the clasp and a curious glance,
Reveals my lost sock, what a strange chance!
A photo of Fido, in costume so grand,
Next to a cake that I built with one hand.

A pinch of nostalgia, a tickle of glee,
Dancing with memories, just my charm and me!
This little round treasure, so hefty with laughs,
Reminds me of moments and my quirky gaffes.

With every small jingle, a chuckle ignites,
Like time travel made easy on those silly nights.
So here's to the charm that holds laughter tight,
For every tear drops, there's a giggle in sight.

Secrets Encased in Gold

Nestled snugly, a glimmering prize,
Hiding truths that provoke big sighs.
Whispers of folly and moments of cheer,
I might find my old lunch, still hiding in here.

A flick of the clasp, and lo! What a mess,
An old ticket stub, and a half-eaten press.
Secrets of snacks and forgotten delights,
Stuck in this trinket, oh how it excites!

A bubblegum wrapper from days gone by,
Sparks of nostalgia make time fly.
Inside this small treasure, my laughter reveals,
The sandwiches, socks, and the joy that it heals.

With each small surprise from the golden surround,
I burst into giggles, what joy I have found!
So here's to the memories locked up so tight,
Each secret, each chuckle, makes everything bright.

Echoes of a Timeless Heart

Tick-tock the moments, treasures galore,
Hiding silly stories I've come to adore.
An echo of laughter, it's timeless, you see,
Packed in this bauble—a riddle of me!

A dance with my dog in a fanciful hat,
Jumps to the beat of a soft, furry brat.
Pictures of chaos, mixed with pure fun,
A time capsule bursting with each little run.

In the clasp of my heart, the silliness lies,
With taffy and mischief spinning like spies.
Each chuckle and giggle, a sweet little part,
In echoes and whispers, beats a merry heart.

So let's open the vault, let the moments flow,
With tales of my life as a foolish show.
In laughter we linger, in joy we take flight,
With echoes that tickle long into the night.

Beneath the Shimmering Surface

Beneath the shine, a charm full of jest,
With secrets and stories, it's simply the best.
A dance card from prom, I'm thinking with glee,
And a rubber ducky says, "Bring on the spree!"

What lies within this glittering case?
A rainbow of moments, all full of grace.
From pies in my face to wild, wacky dreams,
It bursts with the laughter, a joy so it seems.

A sprinkle of nonsense, a dash of delight,
Each pop of surprise makes my heart shine bright.
So here's to the odds, and the goofiness stored,
In this shiny small treasure, life's laughter is poured.

With each twinkling glance, memories resound,
I dance through the stories, new laughter I've found.
So let's jingle our charms, let the fun never cease,
For beneath all the surface, lies pure joy and peace.

A Token of Heartfelt Reverie

In a trinket bright and round,
I found a secret, tightly bound.
A photo of a dog in hats,
Whose owner always fed it rats!

Within the clasp, a note revealed,
"This holds love, if not concealed."
But all I saw was a funny grin,
Of silly pups bound to win!

The heart it kept was surely grand,
Yet more absurd were the demand.
To wear it fondly, they implore,
Even if it means dogs galore!

So now I wear this shiny piece,
With all its wacky memories,
A token of joy, light as air,
A laugh, indeed, beyond compare!

Shrouded in Golden Light

Golden gleams dance on the floor,
A bauble that I can't ignore.
While searching for its ancient lore,
I found my cat still on the chore.

The legend whispered through the years,
Of lovers meeting—with their beers.
But now it holds a goofy tune,
A ringtone stuck for far too soon!

With every laugh beneath its glow,
I question what I really know.
Did Cupid drop his quiver wide,
Or was it just the cat that sighed?

In joy, I wear this shining thing,
A jester's crown, it makes me sing.
For love and laughter intertwined,
In golden shades, the truth's defined!

Timeless Whispers in a Jewel

Oh jewel bright, with tales it brings,
Of foolish pranks and silly flings.
A swirl of whispers, cheeky and bold,
Of all the laughs in memories told.

One lady lost her shoe in dance,
Her name was Marge, she loved romance.
But dancing with a frog, quite rude,
Resulted in a rather odd mood!

The charm declared a love so strange,
With kisses shared, then crazy change.
How many times could one trip fall?
With jewels that giggle, we've seen it all!

In timeless whispers, folly swirls,
Wrapped in love's strange from other worlds,
A jewel of jest, a tale that's bright,
Forever fun in every light!

Chronicles of Love

In pages worn, I did explore,
The chronicles, oh tales of yore.
With hearts and giggles side by side,
A tale of wits, where love collided!

Oh dear, the lovers, what a sight,
Tripped on their dog while in moonlight.
Their kisses caught in sudden flight,
Led to a laugh, an awkward plight!

Across the pages, tales unfold,
Of bumbling hearts and hugs so bold.
For every gaffe, a giggle's birth,
In love we find our endless worth!

So gather 'round, let stories weave,
Of love that's fun, you wouldn't believe!
For in these chronicles, we see,
The joy of life—an absurdity!

Wrapped in Time

A ribbon bright, tied oh so neat,
Wrapped in time, a silly feat.
Inside the box, a prank's delight,
With jokes and jests that feel so right!

A clock that ticks but runs amok,
It shouts, "Eat pie!" with every knock.
Yet here's the kicker, can you guess?
A spoon that sings, can you confess?

In laughter wrapped, each tick invades,
A timepiece filled with wacky shades.
Each moment shared, a funny tale,
Where every hiccup's bound to prevail!

So here's to time, so bright, so bold,
In laughter's arms, love will unfold.
For wrapped in joy, we find the rhyme,
In every jest, we conquer time!

Fragments of Yesterday's Dreams

In a drawer, my memories hide,
Like socks that disappear, oh my!
A tiny key to laughter, perhaps,
Or last night's dinner in a pie.

When I search for treasures, what do I see?
A rubber chicken, quite absurdly.
Its vibrant feathers tickle my mind,
As I reminisce, with joy, I find.

Scattered thoughts like breadcrumbs gone,
Some lost in the toaster, others withdrawn.
A silly tale of forgotten shoes,
Each fragment a giggle, a playful muse.

So here's to dreams in shapes of doubt,
The laughter that echoes when we shout.
In yesterday's chaos, a joke remains,
A dance of the silly runs through our veins.

The Embrace of Forgotten Keepsakes

An old teddy bear with one eye gone,
Still holds secrets of dusk until dawn.
With buttons for eyes and a crooked grin,
He knows all my secrets—time to begin!

In the attic, a hat made for two,
A crown of old pizza, it's all true!
With mushrooms and peppers, we wore it proud,
Befriending the echo, we laughed out loud.

Chasing the relics with whimsical glee,
A sock puppet whispers, 'It's all about me!'
The jester's cap, bright and a sight,
Unfolding tales under beams of light.

So let's toast to treasures that bring out the fun,
In the land of keepsakes, we'll never be done!
With each silly glance, nostalgia takes flight,
In treasures forgotten, we bask in delight.

Unlocking Silent Stories

A tiny box with a squeaky latch,
Holds stories of jest, each one a catch.
Whispers of laughter in every fold,
Like bubbles of soda, sweet and bold.

Inside, I found a lost pair of shoes,
With mismatched socks, colorful hues.
They danced through puddles; oh what a sight!
Unlocking my past with pure delight.

An old sandwich lying side by side,
Saying, 'I'm still here, let's take a ride!'
With crusty laughs and mayonnaise cheer,
Silent stories become quite clear.

Giggling at memories just tucked away,
Unlocking the joy found in yesterday.
In each silly trinket, a tale unfolds,
With laughter and love, our heart it holds.

The Weight of What We Hold

In pockets deep, a treasure trove,
A lost ballpoint pen; will it write or rove?
With tangled string and bits of fluff,
The weight of memories—aren't they tough?

A crumbly cookie that's been there for weeks,
Whispers of chocolate, or maybe just squeaks?
Each bite an adventure, a laugh to behold,
In the weight of our past, stories retold.

With paperclips bent like a gymnast's pose,
We fashion our memories, oh how it goes!
From lunchbox notes to doodles of yore,
The weight of our carries is never a bore.

So let's lighten our hearts and chuckle away,
In the weight of what holds, we find our ballet.
With a wink at the wonders, we joyfully carry,
Each silly glimpse makes our laughter marry.

A Glimpse into Forgotten Tales

In a drawer, where dust balls play,
A locket laughs at yesterday.
It wheezes tales of love and strife,
Like socks that vanish, oh what a life!

A photo slips, a wink, a grin,
How could this guy have ever been?
With curly hair and pants too tight,
A fashion faux pas, what a sight!

Beneath the clasp, a note unfolds,
'You owe me candy!' it boldly scolds.
Sweet tooth tales from schoolyard years,
Yet all I have are chocolate tears.

In laughter's grip, the past we tease,
Echoes of love that never freeze.
With memories scattered far and wide,
We chuckle at the whims of pride!

Heartstrings and Keepsakes

In a box where memories are stored,
A locket giggles, never bored.
It wears a grin, quite bold and cheeky,
As it tells tales that are undeniably sneaky.

Once it sparked joy, but now it's a clown,
With all those secrets just flopping around.
It sways to the rhythm of silly romances,
And bursts into laughter during its dances.

A hidden note says, 'You owe me your fries!'
For lunch dates spent stealing sweet pies.
What a joy to be young and naive,
With promises made that few can believe.

So I cradle this heart that holds the jest,
A keepsake of folly, it's truly the best.
In laughter we find, through all that we keep,
These heartstrings, my friend, are forever a leap!

Echoes of a Timeless Bond

In the attic, the locket grins wide,
With tales of a friendship that's never died.
It swings and sways with a wink in its eye,
As echoes of laughter dance by with a sigh.

One snapshot of Tom with hair like a mop,
Making bubble gum pop with a loud, funny plop.
'We were legends!' it chirps with a flare,
While I cringe at his outfit, a bright purple pair.

An old note spills secrets, all tangled and knotted,
Of pranks gone wrong that we never plotted.
With pizza-filled nights and cartoons till dawn,
The echo grows stronger, never withdrawn.

So we reminisce, through laughter and fun,
While the locket gleams bright like a late evening sun.
These cherished echoes, both goofy and bold,
Tell tales of a bond that will never grow old.

Unraveled Messages of the Past

A trinket sits, so small yet vast,
With unraveling tales meant to last.
It chuckles away as it spins yarns,
Of crushes and dances held in barns.

What once held love now ponders snacks,
Was it cookies or ice cream that first drew our packs?
An accidental spill on a brand new dress,
Causes fits of giggles, such a mess!

A crinkled note reads, 'Meet me at three!'
But what it forgets is that I had to flee.
With sticky fingers and laughter's embrace,
We dashed off forever, a comedic chase!

So here's to the past, with its giggles and glee,
The unraveling truths that still make me see.
With each little secret this trinket reveals,
I'm grateful for laughter and joy that it feels!

Entangled in Whispers of the Past

A trinket found in grandma's drawer,
Tales of mischief, laughter galore.
It chirped like a bird, then fell on the cat,
Now the cat's on a diet, imagine that!

Memories tangled like spaghetti strands,
Running in circles, and taking a stand.
It whispered secrets while I took a nap,
Brought out the polka-dot shorts from the trap!

Old photos jesting, full of delight,
Dancing in socks that were once quite tight.
Echoes of giggles, a puppet on strings,
Who knew my past wore the silliest blings?

The stories it holds, oh, what a delight,
Making me chuckle, oh, what a sight!
Past adventures revealed in a flash,
Who knew nostalgia could cause such a crash!

Chains of Memory

Rusty chains that briefly groan,
Whispering tales of the unknown.
Once a wrist, now a door's delight,
Clanging and banging, fading from sight.

Each link a giggle, a moment, a jest,
Bouncing back laughter, it's simply the best.
Dancing around in the attic's charm,
Clinging to memories, causing no harm.

Caught in the must of forgotten fun,
Linking together, they've barely begun.
Each clink, a reminder, a wink in disguise,
Chains of my youth with such silly ties.

Met with some dust, your cousins all laugh,
Telling me stories, oh what a gaffe!
Now I rediscover, and with glee I see,
Those chains of memory still hold the key!

Bonds of Love

A heart-shaped charm in a drawer so deep,
Echoes of giggles, it's secrets to keep.
Meant for romance, but who needs that?
When all I can think is, "Oh look at that!"

A gift from my crush, or so it was thought,
It's hardly worth it; now look what it caught!
Caught in the couch with a pile of crumbs,
I guess that's what happens when love hums.

Romantic dinners turned into sweet mess,
Bonds of affection often stress and confess.
Yet we still laugh when the past comes around,
With memories made that eternally astound.

So cherish those charms, be they shiny or dull,
For love can be funny, though occasionally dull.
May laughter and joy take the lead in the dance,
In bonds made of humor, we take our chance!

Beneath the Shimmering Surface

A glimmering gem, but what a fake,
Beneath the shine, it was just a mistake.
Polished and glittered, it caught every eye,
But wait till you see it: my how it'll fly!

Underneath layers of bright, shiny dust,
Lay stories of mishaps, and oh, what a bust!
A swim in the fountain, a slip on the floor,
This shiny facade hid many a score.

And yet there it sparkles, with dreams in tow,
A beacon of laughter, putting on a show.
With each little blunder, it laughs and spins,
Beneath the surface, where all the fun begins!

So treasure that glow, even if it's insane,
For under the laughter, there's joy in the pain.
Dare to dive deep, to see what you find,
A humorous treasure that's uniquely designed!

Secrets Worn Close to the Skin

A hidden trinket, snug on my side,
Whispers of secrets, I cannot outride.
Tickling my ear with stories so grand,
Of silly old pranks that went out of hand.

Each loop and twist holds a giggly tale,
Of socks that don't match and a shoe that's gone stale.
Wrapped in my quirks, it zips up tight,
Exposing my laughter, keeping it light.

It knows all the secrets, both funny and weird,
From high-flying jumps to crushes I feared.
Oh, secrets held close with a chuckle and grin,
No one thinks twice at the fun we're all in.

So wear those odd treasures with pride every day,
Laugh at the past as it shows you the way.
Secrets worn snug, beneath skin so thin,
This joyful journey, let the fun begin!

www.ingramcontent.com/pod-product-compliance
Lightning Source LLC
Chambersburg PA
CBHW062107280426
43661CB00086B/298